Steadwell Books World Tour
PHILIPPINES

THOMAS LANG

Raintree

Chicago, Illinois

Copyright Permissions
Raintree
100 N. LaSalle
Suite 1200
Chicago, IL 60602
Customer Service 888-363-4266
Visit our website at www.raintreelibrary.com

Library of Congress Cataloging-in-Publication Data
Lang, Thomas, 1965-
    The Philippines / Thomas Lang.
        p. cm. -- (World tour)
Summary: Describes the history, geography, economy, government, natural resources, landmarks, and culture of the Philippines.
Includes bibliographical references and index.
ISBN 0-7398-6815-2 (Library binding-hardcover)
1. Philippines--Juvenile literature. [1. Philippines.] I. Title. II. Series.
 DS655.L25 2003
 959.9--dc21

                              2003006076

Printed in the United States of America
10 9 8 7 6 5 4 3 2 1 08 07 06 05 04

Photo acknowledgments
Cover (top, L-R) Robertstock Retro File, Paul A. Souders/Corbis; (bottom, L-R) Archive Iconografico, S. A./Corbis, Forden Patrick J./Corbis SYGMA

Title page (L-R) D & R Sullivan/Bruce Coleman Inc., Veronica Garbara/Panos Pictures, North Wind Picture Archives; contents page (L-R) F. Jack Jackson/JACKS/Bruce Coleman Inc., Robertstock Retro File; pp. 5, 21B Carl Roessler/Bruce Coleman Inc.; p. 7 North Wind Picture Archives; p. 8 Stefano Bianchetti/Corbis; pp. 10, 26T Robertstock Retro File; p. 13 F. Jack Jackson/JACKS/Bruce Coleman Inc.; p. 14 Michael Freeman/Bruce Coleman Inc.; p. 15 Reuters NewMedia Inc./Corbis; p. 16 Dallas and John Heaton/Corbis; p. 17 Archive Iconografico, S. A./Corbis; pp. 21T, 40, 44C Mark Downey; pp. 22T, 28 Paul A. Souders/Corbis; p. 22B Joe Galvez; p. 24 D & R Sullivan/Bruce Coleman Inc.; p. 25T Doug Wechsler; pp. 25B, 31B Chris Stowers/Panos Pictures; pp. 26B, 27 George Tapan; p. 29 Ranita Delimont, Agent/OnRequestImages; p. 31T Jeff Foott/Bruce Coleman Inc.; p. 33 Brian J. Coates/Bruce Coleman Inc.; p. 34T Veronica Garbara/Panos Pictures; pp. 34B, 35 Jonah Calinawan/Picture Search; p. 36 Bruce Watkins/Earth Scenes; p. 37 John Borthwick/Lonely Planet Images; p. 39T Gregory G. Dimijian/Photo Researchers, Inc.; p. 39B Albrecht G. Schaefer/Corbis; p. 42 George Gerster/Photo Researchers, Inc.; p. 43T Robert Holmes/Travel Pix; p. 43B Victor Englebert/Picture Search; p. 43B Joe Galvez/Picture Search; p. 44T Alain Nogues/Corbis SYGMA; 44B Bruce Glikas/NewsCom.

Photo research by Amor Montes de Oca

CONTENTS

The Philippines's Past 6

The Philippines's Geography 10

Manila: A Big-City Snapshot 16

4 Top Sights 20

Going to School in the Philippines . . . 28

Filipino Sports 29

From Farming to Factories 30

The Filipino Government 32

Religions of the Philippines 33

Filipino Food 34

Cookbook 35

Up Close: The Island of Mindoro 36

Holidays 40

Learning the Language 41

Quick Facts 42

People to Know 44

More to Read 45

Glossary 46

Index 48

Welcome to the Philippines

Are you interested in the Philippines? The best way to learn about this fascinating country is to go there. Get to know this nation by walking its city streets, eating fresh food at local restaurants, and touring through its hidden fishing villages.

If you cannot get to the Philippines, this book will help satisfy your curiosity. The next best thing to visiting a foreign country is to read about one!

So whether you are planning a visit or you just want to learn about the Philippines, read on.

Some Tips to Get You Started:

• *Use the Table of Contents*

In this kind of book, there may be some sections that interest you more than others. Take a look at the Contents. Pick the chapters that interest you and start with those. Check out the other chapters later.

• *Use the Glossary*

When you see **bold** words in the text, you can look them up in the Glossary. The Glossary will help you learn their meanings.

• *Use the Index*

Looking for specific information? Look in the Index. There you will find a list of the subjects covered in the book and the pages where they can be found.

▲CORAL REEFS, PHILIPPINES
The coral reefs that lie off the shores of many of the Philippine islands are some of the most beautiful in the world. Many of these reefs are in danger of being destroyed completely from fishing, tourists, and pollution.

THE PHILIPPINES'S PAST

The first stop on your tour of the Philippines should be a look at this country's past. The Philippines has played a fascinating role in world history.

Ancient History

Historians think that people showed up in the Philippines about 30,000 years ago. The ancestors of today's Filipinos came from the Malay **Peninsula** (now Malaysia and Thailand). That was about 5,000 years ago. Some of these groups of people ventured inland, instead of just living on the coast. Because the Philippines is made up of many islands, most of these groups lived apart from each other. Each developed its own society. One thing they had in common was a similar language. Most spoke a form of Malay. Modern Filipino comes from this language.

The Colonial Era

In the 1300s, the Ming **Dynasty** in China decided to claim the Philippine islands. But the Philippines were far away from China's capital and difficult to manage. The Ming Dynasty quickly gave up its plans.

In 1521, the explorer Ferdinand Magellan arrived in the Philippines, but was killed in a battle between his soldiers and the local population. When the Spanish returned in 1565, they were able to form a permanent settlement. The settlers claimed the islands for Spain, and called them the Philippines after King Philip II of Spain. For the next 333 years, Spain would rule over the country.

▲ MOUNT MAYON
This painting depicts an ancient native village at the base of Mt. Mayon, one of the Philippines most active volcanoes.

Struggle for Independence

Filipinos were not very happy with these new conquerers. They were basically enslaved by the Spanish.

Spain used the Philippines for trade. As the economy of the Philippines grew, so did the desires of Filipinos to be free from Spanish colonial rule. By the end of the 1800s, Filipinos started demanding change.

In the 1890s, the United States came to the Filipinos' aid. On June 12, 1898, a Filipino leader named Emilio Aguinaldo declared the Philippines independent. By August, the Filipinos and the Americans had chased Spain out of the area.

Unfortunately, after Spain left, the United States decided it wanted the Philippines for itself. Rather than freeing the country, the United States claimed the islands as its own property. Instead of becoming free, the Philippines just got a new ruler.

The Philippines and the United States

In 1935 the Philippines became a **commonwealth** of the United States. That meant that the Philippines ruled over itself, but that the United States government was in charge of its military and international politics.

On December 10, 1941, Japan attacked the Philippines. It was just three days after the Japanese attack on Pearl Harbor and the beginning of World War II. For the next

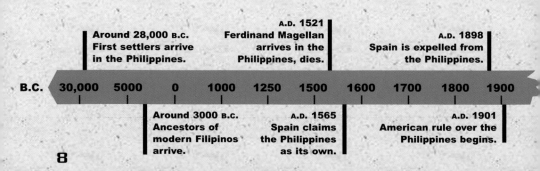

Around 28,000 B.C.
First settlers arrive
in the Philippines.

A.D. 1521
Ferdinand Magellan
arrives in the
Philippines, dies.

A.D. 1898
Spain is expelled from
the Philippines.

| B.C. | 30,000 | 5000 | 0 | 1000 | 1250 | 1500 | 1600 | 1700 | 1800 | 1900 |

Around 3000 B.C.
Ancestors of
modern Filipinos
arrive.

A.D. 1565
Spain claims
the Philippines
as its own.

A.D. 1901
American rule over the
Philippines begins.

three years, the United States and the Philippines fought side by side against the Japanese. In 1944, the Japanese were defeated. Two years later, in 1946, the Philippines was granted complete independence from the United States.

The Philippines Today

Since World War II, the country managed to rebuild and established a working **democracy.** Since 1946, the Philippines has prospered.

The Philippines experienced one rough patch after 1946. From 1965 to 1986, the Philippines struggled with a corrupt leader named Ferdinand Marcos. Marcos cheated in elections and stole money from the Filipino people.

In 1986, Marcos fled the country after people started demanding that he step down. A new leader named Corazon Aquino took over. Since then, the Philippines has been one of the most stable and democratic countries in Asia.

A.D. 1935
Philippines becomes a commonwealth under United States protection.

A.D. 1944
Japan defeated in the Philippines.

A.D. 1965
Marcos dictatorship begins.

A.D. 1986
Marcos dictatorship ends, Aquino presidency begins.

1920   1930   1940   1950   1960   1970   1980   1990   2000   **A.D.**

A.D. 1941
Japan attacks the Philippines.

A.D. 1946
The Philippines granted total independence.

9

THE PHILIPPINES'S GEOGRAPHY

If you visited one island a day, it would take you about 20 years to visit all of the islands in the Philippines. Some are pretty small, but others are very large and covered with bustling cities and remote forests.

Land

The Philippines lies north and east of Indonesia and Malaysia and south of China. The Philippines does not share any of its islands with other countries. That means there are no borders.

The Philippines is divided into three main groups of islands. The northern group consists of two large islands: Luzon and Mindoro. The central group is called the Visayan Islands and consists of nearly 7,000 small islands. The southern group includes the large island of Mindanao and the Sulu **Archipelago.**

The islands extend about 1,150 miles (1,850 km) from north to south and about 600 miles (965 km) from west to east. The entire coastline measures 22,550 miles (36,289 km).

The inland areas of most islands in the Philippines are mountainous. The highest peak is on the island of Mindanao. It is called Mount Apo and is 9,692 feet (2,954 m) high.

► MT. APO
This ancient and majestic mountain is considered the "grandfather" of Philippine peaks.

▶ PHILIPPINES'S SIZE

The Philippines takes up an area of 115,831 square miles (300,000 sq km). It is just slightly larger than the state of Arizona.

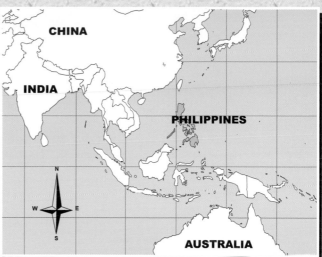

Water

The Philippines is surrounded by four main bodies of water. The Luzon Strait is to the north, the South China Sea is to the west, to the east lies the Pacific Ocean, and to the south is the Celebes Sea.

Because the Philippines is made up of islands, there are not many long rivers. The longest is on the island of Luzon. It is called the Cagayan and is only 200 miles (322 km) long.

Luzon Strait

South China Sea

Philippine Sea

Manila

Philippine Trench

Celebes Sea

THE PHILIPPINES

★ National Capital
— Rivers

▶ **PHILIPPINES TRENCH**
This underwater trench is located in the Pacific Ocean and is one of the deepest points in the world, at 34,440 feet (10,497 m) deep.

▲ FUN IN THE SUN
Because the Philippines is made up of so many islands,
the country has a lot of beaches. Tourists come year round
to relax and enjoy the sunny weather.

Weather

The Philippines is a **tropical** country and is warm and wet. There are three seasons in the Philippines: the rainy season (June to October), the cool season (November to February), and the hot season (March to May).

Temperatures can rise to 100°F (38°C) in the hot season. In the cool and rainy season, the temperatures get down to 70°F (21°C). The average yearly temperature is 80°F (27°C).

▲ RICE TERRACES OF LUZON
A shortage of flat land has made it necessary for farmers to use some mountainsides and hills for growing crops. These rice terraces in Luzon are world famous for their exceptional height.

▲ **DON'T FORGET YOUR UMBRELLA!**
Because of the Philippines's tropical climate, the country gets a lot of rainfall. These cars are driving though a flooded street in the Philippine capital city of Manila.

MANILA: A BIG-CITY SNAPSHOT

▲ PORT OF MANILA
It is thought that the port of Manila, located at the mouth of the Pasig River, was founded around the 12th century. Today, more than 13 million people call this capital city their home.

The Philippines is famous for its gentle shores, quiet fishing villages, and endless forests. It also has always been known as a **multicultural** nation. No place shows this more than Manila.

The Intramuros

Tragically, much of Manila was destroyed in World War II. Still, a few of the oldest sights remain, and much has been rebuilt since the war's end.

The Intramuros is a walled section of the city built by the Spanish hundreds of years ago. It is the oldest part of Manila and is filled with treasures from the past. Start your visit at Fort Santiago at the mouth of the Pasig River. The Intramuros was designed to protect invaders from Manila. This fort was a great place to fire cannons at enemy ships trying to sneak up the river.

Next, walk to the San Augustin Church. This church was built in 1599 and has a great museum where you can learn about Catholicism in the Philippines.

After visiting the church, walk over to the Cultural Center of the Philippines. This center focuses on Filipino art and culture. If you time your visit right, you might be able to see a play or listen to some live music.

Rizal Park

At the far end of the Intramuros, you will find Rizal Park. This park was named after Jose Rizal, who was a hero in the Philippines' struggle against Spain.

The park is a great place to kick back and relax. But if you want a more active day, you can

▶ **FORT SANTIAGO**
Fort Santiago was built in the 1500s. It served as the military headquarters for the Spanish, British, American, and Japanese regimes when they occupied the country.

visit the Museum of the Filipino People. It is right in the park, and it will give you a great understanding of the history and culture of the Filipinos.

The park is also a great place to eat lunch. Buy some pork dumplings from a streetside vendor and sit under a tree. While you eat, you can take some time to people-watch.

Beyond the Old Town

One place to visit is Chinatown. Many Chinese settled in Manila long ago. They have influenced much of the local culture, especially the food. Plan your visit to Chinatown around lunchtime. You can sit and eat in a restaurant, or just stop at streetside stands along Chinatown's bustling streets. Many Filipinos head to Chinatown for the food and the shopping, so you will not be alone. You can also pick up a few souvenirs for friends here. The shops sell everything from herbal medicines to gold earrings.

If you have not had enough shopping, head to the famous Carriedo Street Market. Be prepared to push your way through crowds of people. This is where Filipinos head to bargain hunt for things like fresh fruit, stereos, and designer clothing. An afternoon at this market will remind you that Manila is more than just museums and historical sights. Bring your appetite—this is the perfect place to grab a nice piece of fish and a bowl of rice!

MANILA'S TOP-10 CHECKLIST

Still not sure how to plan your trip? Here's a list of things to do in Manila.

☐ Take a tour of Fort Santiago.

☐ Spend the morning walking along the ancient walls of the Intramuros.

☐ Wander around the San Augustin Church.

☐ Check out the colonial art in the San Augustin Church Museum.

☐ See the symphony at the Cultural Center of the Philippines.

☐ Visit the Jose Rizal memorial in Rizal park.

☐ Get some pork dumplings or grilled fish from a vendor and eat it under a tree in Rizal Park.

☐ Wander the busy streets of Chinatown.

☐ Eat some halo halo (a delicious mixture of fruit and ice cream) at the Carriedo Street Market.

☐ Buy souvenirs at the market for friends back home.

FASCINATING FACT

The Philippines is home to the world's smallest fish. It's called the Pandaka Pygmea and it's only about half an inch long (about 1.2 centimeters). The fish live in small streams and rivers. If you want to see one, be prepared for lots of searching. Not only are they tiny, but also their bodies are transparent—that means you can see right through them!

Hundred Islands National Park

One of the Philippines's main attractions is its beaches. The Philippines has thousands of miles of unspoiled beachfront. Sometimes this means busy beach towns with restaurants and merry-go-rounds. Most of the time, however, it means solitude and peace on deserted sandy shores.

One of the best places to explore the Philippines's ocean environment is Hundred Islands National Park. It is on the north end of Luzon Island and makes for a perfect weekend trip from Manila.

Hundred Islands National Park is made up of more than 100 small islands. Most are huge **coral** and rock towers that stick out of the water. Other small islands have sandy beaches. Rent a boat and spend the morning exploring this mysterious and beautiful water paradise. Stop at one of the beaches for a picnic and a nap in the sun. If you still have energy, you can hire a guide to take you **snorkeling** through the surrounding underwater coral formations.

FASCINATING FACTS

1. The Philippines is the third largest English-speaking country in the world.

2. The Philippines is nicknamed "The Pearls of the Orient" because the long line of scattered islands looks like pearls.

3. The world's biggest school is in the Philippines. Close to 25,000 students (kindergarten through 12th grade) are enrolled!

▼ A NATURAL PARADISE

Hundred Islands National Park was established in 1940. At the entrance stands the Philippines's oldest lighthouse. Historians believe that it was once powered by coconut oil!

◀ CELEBRATION!
The Ati-Atihan Festival is one of the most beloved celebrations in the Philippines. Headdresses and costumes are made of a variety of items, like shells, feathers, bamboo, plant leaves, flowers, beads, and an assortment of pieces of glass, metals, and plastics.

The Ati-Atihan Festival

The Philippines is made up of many ethnic minorities. One group is called the Ati. Legend says that ten Ati princes from the nearby island of Borneo first came to Panay island in A.D. 1212. They struck a deal with the local ruler of the island and were allowed to stay. Ever since, the Ati have celebrated the deal with a huge festival called Ati-Atihan, which means "be like the Atis."

Ati-Atihan is held in the town of Kalibo on the island of Panay. The festival lasts for days, but the main event is always on the third Sunday of January. If you can, try to include it on your trip. You won't be disappointed.

One of the main attractions of the festival is what people wear. People paint their faces, wear sparkling jewelry, and dress up in elaborate costumes. Kalibo is also filled with street performers, singers, drummers, dancers, and thousands of other people there to have a great time.

The other thing you will do a lot of at Ati-Atihan is eat. The local food is delicious, and when you see all the grilled shrimp and fried dumplings being served, you might not be able to help yourself. Dig in!

Mt. Apo

You may think that the Philippines is just one big coastline, but it has several large mountain ranges as well. The tallest mountain in the Philippines is Mount Apo on the southern island of Mindanao.

Mt. Apo is 9,692 feet (2,954 m) tall, so be prepared for some serious hiking. It often takes a few days to get to the top of this mountain.

Mt. Apo is an inactive volcano, so there are many interesting things to see on your way to the top. You will see geysers, natural hot springs, strange sulfur formations, and rock craters. There is also a lot of wildlife to see. If you are lucky, you will spot a Philippine eagle soaring above one of Mt. Apo's rock cliffs.

If you don't see any eagles, don't worry. After heading to the peak, you can visit the Philippine Eagle Breeding Station, not far from the mountain. Here you can see all the eagles you want.

◄ EAGLE EYED
Mt. Alpo is home to the country's national bird, the Philippine eagle. Because humans are taking over much of its habitat, this bird is dangerously close to disappearing off the earth.

◀ **MT. APO**
Mt. Apo is
Southeast Asia's
second highest
mountain. Drill
holes are often
tested on this
inactive moun-
tain's geysers
and hot springs.

◀ **FESTIVAL**
These Marawians are dressed in traditional costumes made of muslin. Muslin is a type of light cotton cloth.

▶ **MARAWI MOSQUE**
The population of Marawi is 90% Muslim.

Town of Marawi

Before the Spanish came to the Philippines, Muslim traders established settlements there. Today, there are still large Muslim areas in the Philippines' south. The center of Muslim life in this area is the town of Marawi.

Because the Philippines is primarily Christian, Marawi will seem like a very different place. There are mosques instead of churches, people dress differently, and pork will not be the main dish at dinner time.

Since it is so different from the rest of the Philippines, Marawi is a great place to see firsthand the diversity of the Philippines. It is in a beautiful location, surrounded by hills and right on Lake Lanao. If you make it to Marawi, be sure to visit the King Faisel **Mosque** and the Aga Khan Museum. The mosque will give you a great sense of the Filipino-Muslim way of life. The museum will teach you about the history of Muslims in the Philippines.

One of the problems in Marawi is that it has become a dangerous place to visit in recent years. Some Filipino Muslims want to start their own Muslim country around Marawi. This has led to fighting in parts of the region. Almost everyone you will meet in Marawi will be kind and welcoming, but it is best to be careful when traveling in this area.

▲ **LAKE LANAO**
Marawi City sits on the shores of Lake Lanao. This lake is the second largest in the country, covering 137 square miles (357 sq km).

GOING TO SCHOOL IN THE PHILIPPINES

◄ **SCHOOL'S IN SESSION**
Filipino children study the same kind of courses students do in the U.S., like math, science, and reading.

Filipino children are required to go to elementary school until they are twelve years old. Many continue with school past that age. They go to secondary schools (like junior high and high schools). Many students then go on to college. The Philippines has a very high **literacy** rate, with 96% of the population knowing how to read and write.

Classes in the Philippines are taught in three different languages. In the first two years of elementary school, lessons are taught in the local language. After that, classes are taught in both English and Filipino. The higher the grade, the more likely the class will be taught in English. Most college classes are taught in English.

Most students in the Philippines attend government schools, which are free. However, many students go to private schools. Many of these private schools are also Roman Catholic.

Obviously, water sports are popular in the Philippines. It is, after all, an island nation. Filipinos like to sail, swim, and scuba dive. If you visit one of the major resort areas, you can rent a boat or just paddle around in the surf. If you are more adventurous, you can get a guide to take you diving in one of the Philippines's many spectacular coral reefs.

As far as team sports go, you won't find anything more popular in the Philippines than basketball. There are amateur leagues all around the country, so you can always find a game to watch. And since there are basketball hoops on nearly every playground, you can also join in a game with the locals if you feel like it.

One of the most unique sports in the Philippines is jai alai (pronounced "hi-a-lye"). Jai alai is a little like racquetball. Four players bounce a rubber ball against a wall and try to catch it again in wicker baskets, called cestas. This sport is not for the timid. The ball can go as fast as 150 miles (240 km)per hour!

▶ **SURF'S UP!**
You can imagine how popular water sports are to Filipinos!

FROM FARMING TO FACTORIES

About half of the people in the Philippines make their living as farmers. They grow crops and raise animals for both food and income.

The main crop Filipinos grow is rice. Rice is the essential food in every Filipino meal. Farmers also grow things like potatoes, bananas, and coconuts. They raise animals like pigs and chicken for meat.

Filipinos eat many of their farm products fresh. Factories also turn these materials into food products (for instance, canned coconut milk). Farmers also may have fisheries where they raise fish and shrimp.

A lot of Filipinos fish in the ocean for a living. They catch everything from crabs to anchovies to tuna. Some of the fish is eaten fresh, while much of it is packaged and sold around the world.

Many people in the Philippines work in factories. The Philippines is famous for producing fabrics and clothes. Check the tags on your clothes—chances are you have something made in the Philippines hanging in your closet. Filipino factories also produce things like chemicals and electronics.

Mining is also an important part of the Filipino **economy.** Copper and gold are the most important minerals found in the Philippines. In addition, lumber is a major Filipino product. Many people work in the forests to bring wood to people in the Philippines and around the world. The Philippines is most famous for a rare and valuable kind of hardwood called **mahogany.**

▲ **FISHING AT A COST**
While many Filipinos rely on fishing for a living, scientists are very concerned that fishing and pollution are destroying the Philippines's coral reefs.

►**MAKATI BUSINESS DISTRICT, MANILA**
This section of Manila is the premier financial district in the Philippines.

And of course, many Filipinos have the kind of jobs that keep any society running. They practice medicine, teach school, drive trucks, and do all the other jobs that any country needs to survive.

THE FILIPINO GOVERNMENT

The Philippines is a democracy. That means that people chose their own leaders in elections.

The national Filipino government has three main divisions: the president, the senate, and the house of representatives. The president serves one 6-year term. He or she helps make the laws that govern the Philippines. The current president of the Philippines is Gloria Macapagal-Arroyo.

There are 24 senators in the Philippines, each serving terms that last six years. There are 254 members of the house of representatives. The house and senate work with the president to make the country's laws.

The Philippines is divided into 73 smaller **provinces,** and each has its own governor. There are also 60 independent cities that are governed by mayors.

THE PHILIPPINES' FLAG

Filipinos have a very interesting flag. The white triangle on the flag stands for **fraternity** and equality. The blue field stands for peace, truth, and justice. The red field stands for patriotism and bravery. The three stars stand for Luzon Island, Mindanao Island, and the Visayas Islands. The eight rays of the sun symbolize the first eight provinces of the Philippines.

RELIGIONS OF THE PHILIPPINES

◀ LUZON
This is a Spanish-era Catholic church on the island of Luzon. Catholicism has been practiced in the Philippines since the 16th century.

More than 90% of the people in the Philippines are Christian. Most of these Christians are also Roman Catholic. Roman Catholicism was brought to the Philippines by the Spanish in the 1500s. A smaller number of Filipino Christians are Protestants.

The Philippines has its own form of Christianity, called the Aglipayan Church. This church was founded in 1902 because some Filipinos had grown tired of foreigners telling them how to worship. The church was very popular at first, but today only 3% of the population is Aglipayan.

About 5% of the people in the Philippines are Muslim. Muslims worship one god named Allah and follow the teachings of a prophet named Mohammed. Mohammed's teachings are found in a holy book called the Koran.

FILIPINO FOOD

Since the Philippines is a country with more than 7,000 islands, fish is one of the main ingredients in Filipino food. Whether it is a tuna steak or grilled shrimp, you can be sure that fish in this country is as fresh as it can be. The only thing more common here than fish is rice. You will probably eat it at every meal.

Filipinos also eat a lot of meat. Pork is the most common, and Filipinos have countless ways to cook it. It is grilled, fried, baked, and sometimes stewed in ginataan, which is a sauce made from coconut milk. If it is a special occasion, like a wedding, they might roast a whole pig.

If you prefer non-meat dishes, try the cassava, which is a kind of starchy root vegetable that some say tastes like a melon. It is one of the most popular foods in the Philippines. You also might want to try the eggplant and potato dishes, served up in a creamy ginataan.

◀ SAVE ROOM FOR DESSERT!
If you are a dessert-lover, make sure to try the halo halo. This after-dinner sweet is made from crushed ice, condensed milk, and lots of fruit. One of the most unusual ingredients of halo halo is red beans.

FILIPINO FRUIT PUDDING

If you are looking for a great treat on
a hot day, try this cold fruit pudding.
It is a Filipino favorite. It is a perfect dessert
for a summer meal and it makes
a great snack.

Ingredients:
3 cups heavy cream
16 ounces cream cheese
6 12-ounce cans of fruit cocktail, drained
2 12-ounce cans of cubed pineapple, drained
2 cups shredded coconut
16 ounces chopped, unsalted almonds
3 cups diced apples

Directions:
• Mix the cream cheese and heavy cream
until smooth.
• Mix the fruit, coconut, and almonds.
• Combine the cream cheese mixture with the fruit.
• Chill in the refrigerator for 12 hours.

WARNING:
**Never cook or bake by yourself. Always have an adult
assist you in the kitchen.**

UP CLOSE: THE ISLAND OF MINDORO

A good way to get to know the Philippines is to pick a spot and explore it thoroughly. One of the best places to pick is the island of Mindoro. This island is just to the south of Luzon. It is the seventh largest island in the Philippines, so you will not run out of things to do, but it is small enough that you can really get to know it.

One of the most interesting things on Mindoro Island are its many traditional peoples. The island's original inhabitants are called the Mangyans. There are several **subgroups** of Mangyans and they live in small settlements throughout Mindoro.

One of the most interesting groups of Mangyans is called the Hanunoo. There are about 13,000 on the island and they are famous for their poetry and music. They play guitars and nose flutes (flutes you play by blowing air out of your nose!), and sing songs written on pieces of bamboo. Most make their living through farming. They grow things like rice, beans, sweet potatoes, and sugar cane.

▶ **MINDORO ISLAND**
This popular tourist spot was once the site of a sea landing by U.S. forces in World War II.

► **PUERTO GALERO**
This beach offers excellent sailing
and snorkeling opportunities.

Bulalacao

Some say the best Hanunoo village to visit is Bulalacao, in the south of Mindoro. If you make it to Bulalacao, you can spend the day listening to traditional music, eating delicious rice dishes, and buying clothing and baskets from Hanunoo artists.

Puerto Galera

There are plenty of interesting things to see on Mindoro. But one of the main reasons people come here is for the beach. Don't feel bad for wanting to spend all day lying in white sand and swimming in crystal-clear water. It doesn't mean you aren't learning. This island is one of the wonders of the natural world. Take in the sea and sun and marvel at the fascinating underwater creatures.

The best beach area in Mindoro is a town called Puerto Galera. This town is in the northeast part of the island. Lots of people come down from Manila to surf and snorkel here. If you like crowded beach towns with plenty of activity, this is the place for you. Relax in the sun and then cool off with a big bowl of halo halo— a sort of Filipino fruit ice cream. Some people prefer Tamaraw Beach just up the coast. It has all the surf and sand, but is not as crowded.

Environment in the Extreme

In search of something a little more exciting than napping in the sun? Head to the city of San Jose, hire a guide, and head to Apo Reef National Park. If you have been properly trained to do so, this is the best place to snorkel and scuba dive in the Philippines. You will be amazed by the endless coral maze that seems to go on forever and the countless colorful fish.

The Mount Iglit/Mount Baco National Wildlife Sanctuary has its charms, too. It is not far from San Jose and well worth a trip. You can see wild buffalo, Philippine eagles, and more snakes and lizards than you can count.

▲ MORAY EEL
There are about 100 species of moray eels worldwide. These fish live in coral reefs or rocky areas of tropical seas worldwide, like the Philippines's Apo Reef National Park.

► WILD BUFFALO
This wild buffalo, also known as a tamaraw, lives safely inside the Mount Iglit/Mount Baco National Wildlife Sanctuary in the Philippines. It can weigh up to 660 pounds (300 kg).

HOLIDAYS

Most people in the Philippines are Roman Catholic. Because of this, Filipinos celebrate many Christian holidays.

The most important Christian holidays are Easter and Christmas. Easter marks the death and resurrection of Jesus. It is usually celebrated with large feasts, religious services, and parades where Filipinos wear colorful masks. People also perform small plays that re-enact the death of Jesus.

Christmas, which commemorates the birth of Jesus, is celebrated with large meals with family and friends. Filipinos are known for making colorful lanterns to display at Christmas time. One of the most important Christmas traditions in the Philippines is mass, or religious service, held at church. This service is called Misas de Aguinaldo, and usually begins at four in the morning with people walking through the streets singing Christmas songs.

There are two important national holidays in the Philippines: Labor Day and Independence Day. Labor Day is on May 1 and celebrates Filipino workers. Independence Day is on June 12. This holiday celebrates the day in 1898 when the Philippines ended 333 years of Spanish rule. People also celebrate this holiday with political rallies, firecrackers, and concerts.

▶ FILIPINO INDEPENDENCE DAY CELEBRATION
Filipinos celebrate their Independence Day much like we do, with parades that commemorate the heroes who died for their country.

LEARNING THE LANGUAGE

English	Filipino	How to Say It
Yes	oo	OO
No	hindî	hin-DEE
My name is ...	Akó si	ak-OH si
Thank You	salámat	sa-LA-mat
Hello	kumusta	KOO-moo-sta
Goodbye	paalam	PAH-ah-lam
I'm sorry	Sori hô	SOH-ri HO
The Philippines	Pilipinas	PILI-pee-nas

QUICK FACTS

PHILIPPINES

Capital ▶
Manila

Borders
Luzon Strait (N)
Pacific Ocean (E)
Celebes Sea (S)
South China Sea (W)

Area
115,830 sq miles
(300,000 sq km)

Population
78,000,000

Natural Resources
Manganese, gold,
magnetite,
hydroelectric power

Major Industries
Textiles and clothing,
food processing,
sugar production,
electronics manufacturing

Aglipayan
(an independent church)
3%

Protestant
8%

Muslim
5%

Other
1%

**Roman
Catholic
83%**

◀ **Religions**

Largest Cities
Manila (13,503,000)
Cebu (1,198,000)
Davao (1,170,000)

Chief Crops
Rice, coconuts,
bananas, sugar

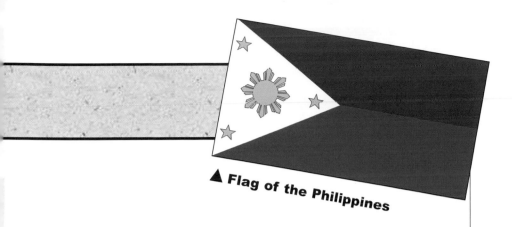

▲ **Flag of the Philippines**

Longest River
Cagayan River
200 miles (322 km)

Coastline ▶
22,550 miles
(36,289 km)

Natural Resources
Coal, oil, copper, silver
gold, lumber

Literacy Rate
96% of Filipinos
can read and write

◀ **Monetary Unit**
Peso

PEOPLE TO KNOW

◀ FERDINAND MARCOS

Ferdinand Marcos served as the president of the Philippines for over 30 years. He was notorious for his brutality and for stealing money from the Filipino people. His dictatorship lasted from 1965 to 1986, when a popular uprising forced him to flee to the United States. Ferdinand Marcos was born on September 11, 1917. He died on September 28, 1989.

▶ CORAZON AQUINO

Many say that Corazon Aquino was the Philippines' most important leader. She became president in 1986 and helped the Philippines recover from 30 years of dictatorship under Ferdinand Marcos. She left office in 1992 and is still active in Filipino politics today. Corazon Aquino was born on January 25, 1933.

◀ LEA SALONGA

Lea Salonga started out singing professionally at 7, and by age 10 had cut a gold record. Today, Salonga plays all around the world and is famous in the United States for her starring roles on Broadway. Lea is best known as the voice of Princess Jasmine in Disney's *Aladdin*. Her hit song from this animated movie, *A Whole New World,* even won an Oscar! Lea Salonga was born on February 22, 1971.

MORE TO READ

Would you like to read more about the Philippines? Check out these books below.

Davis, Lucille. *The Philippines.* Mankato, Minn.: Bridgestone Books, 1999.

If you are looking for a general book about the Philippines, check out this one. It is full of useful information.

Lucas, Alice (editor), Carl Angel (illustrator). *Mga Kuwentong Bayan: Folk Stories from the Philippines.* San Francisco: Many Cultures Publishing, 1995.

This book will give you a good sense of the traditions and history of the Philippines as seen through its folk tales.

Nickles, Greg. *Philippines—The People.* New York: Crabtree Publishing, 2002.

This book focuses on the most interesting aspect of the Philippines—its people!

Sullivan, Margaret, and Mike Downey (photographer). *The Philippines: Pacific Crossroads.* Dillon Press, 1998.

With its Spanish and American influences, the Philippines is a truly international country. Learn how the Philippines fits into the larger world with this excellent book.

GLOSSARY

Archipelago—a group of islands

Cassava—a starchy root used in many types of Filipino cooking

Colonial—referring to a situation where one country is controlled by another

Commonwealth—when two or more countries work together

Coral—a hard material made of the skeletons of tiny ocean creatures

Democracy—a form of government where people elect their leaders by vote

Dictatorship—a type of government where one ruler has complete control over a country

Dynasty—a series of leaders from the same family

Economy—all issues dealing with a country's finances

Fraternity—loyalty and friendship between people

Literacy—the ability to read and write

Mahogany—a kind of rare, hardwood

Mosque—a place where Muslims go to worship

Multicultural—containing many groups of people from different cultures

Peninsula—an area of land almost entirely surrounded by water

Province—a region of a country

Settler—a person who moves to a new place

Snorkeling—swimming using a bent plastic tube to breathe under water

Subgroup—a small group of people within a larger group of people

Tropical—an area characterized as being hot and having much rainfall

INDEX

Aglipayan Church 33
Aguinaldo, Emilio 7
Aquino, Corazon 9
Ati-Atihan Festival 23

basketball 29
beaches 20, 37–38
Bulalacao 37

Cagayan River 12
China, Chinese 6, 18
commonwealth 8
coral reefs 20, 29, 38

ethnic peoples 6, 16, 18, 23,
    26–27, 36, 37

farming 30, 36
fish 30, 34, 38
forests 10, 16, 30

Hundred Islands National Park
    20

islands 6, 10, 12, 20, 23, 29, 34,
    36–38

jai alai 29
Japan 8–9

Luzon Island 10, 12, 20

Macapagal-Arroyo, Gloria 32
Magellan, Ferdinand 6
Malay 6
Manila 16–18, 20
Marawi 26–27
Mindanao 10, 24
Mindoro 10, 36–38
Mount Apo 10, 24
Muslims 26, 27, 33

Philip II (king) 6
Puerto Galera 38

rice 18, 30, 34, 36, 37
Roman Catholicism 17, 28, 33,
    40

Spain, Spanish 6, 7–8, 17, 26,
    33, 40

United States 7–9

wildlife 24, 30, 34, 38
World War II 9, 17